Moa, *the largest bird that ever lived (now extinct)*

South American bird-eating spider, *the largest type of spider*

Every year millions of people come to the Natural History Museum to discover the world of animals, plants and minerals. It has always been famous for its dinosaur remains and lifesize model of a blue whale. But today there are also some exciting new exhibitions, with computer games to play and films to watch.

In this book you can find out more about the Museum and what goes on behind the scenes...

Acknowledgments

The publishers and author would like to thank the Museum staff for their help and advice, and the following for permission to use illustrative material:
British Museum (Natural History), title page and pages 4 (top), 7 (bottom), 10, 15 (bottom right), 24-25 (black and white), 40 (bottom); J Allan Cash Photolibrary, page 42 (top right); R W Ditchfield, illustration on pages 5, 50-51; Mike Gordon, illustration on pages 40-41, 45; Frank Greenaway, pages 34 (left), 35 (top); Robert Harding Picture Library, page 43 (top); Arthur Hayward, pages 11, 12, 13 (top); Adam Hook, illustration on page 43; Colin Keates, pages 5 (bottom left), 33 (bottom), 38, 39, 42 (left), 48, 49, back endpaper A (top right and bottom); David Morbey, cover, front endpaper and pages 4-5 (bottom), 5, 6, 7 (top), 8, 9, 13 (bottom), 14, 15 (top and bottom left), 16-23, 24 (inset), 26-29, 30 (bottom), 31 (bottom), 32, 33 (top), 34 (right), 35 (bottom), 36, 37, 40 (top), 41, 43 (bottom), 44-47, back endpaper A (top left), back endpaper B; Rida, pages 30 (top by Richard Moody), 31 (top and bottom right by David Bayliss); Phil Weare, illustration on front endpaper and pages 6, 32.
Book and cover design by R W Ditchfield.

British Library Cataloguing in Publication Data

Wilson, Karena
    Discovering the Natural History Museum.
    1. London. Kensington and Chelsea (London Borough).
    Museums : British Museum (Natural History)
    I. Title   II. Series
    508′.074′02134
    ISBN 0-7214-1181-9

First edition

Published by Ladybird Books Ltd Loughborough Leicestershire UK
Ladybird Books Inc Auburn Maine 04210 USA

© LADYBIRD BOOKS LTD MCMLXXXIX

Printed in England

DISCOVERING
THE NATURAL HISTORY MUSEUM

written by KARENA WILSON

Ladybird Books

How the Museum began

Sir Hans Sloane was a famous doctor who loved to collect things. In his animal collection alone there were 1886 mammals, 1172 birds, 1555 fishes and 5439 insects.

When Sir Hans died in 1752, at the age of 92, he left his famous collection to the British

Sir Hans Sloane

people. At first it was kept in a new museum, called the *British Museum*, but soon the museum became too crowded. The **natural history** objects needed another home...

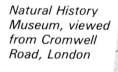

Natural History Museum, viewed from Cromwell Road, London

Carved Nautilus shell, from Sloane's original collection

The Natural History Museum building

A famous architect from Liverpool, called Alfred Waterhouse, was chosen to design a new *Natural History Museum*. Waterhouse wanted his building to be very grand so he designed it to look like a cathedral, with high ceilings, columns and stained glass windows.

*A kind of pottery, called **terracotta**, was used to build the Museum and to make the many decorative animal and plant mouldings*

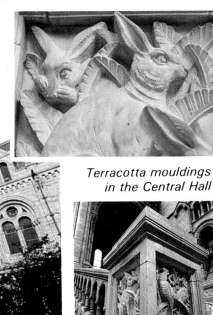

Terracotta mouldings in the Central Hall

Where the specimens come from

In the Museum today, there are thousands of **specimens** on display for visitors to see – from huge dinosaur skeletons to tiny insects. Some of the specimens come from Sir Hans Sloane's original collection but most have been added in the last hundred years, from many different sources.

When people find unusual natural objects they often bring them to the Museum for experts to identify. Some of the very rare specimens on display today were just lucky finds!

In January 1983, Mr William Walker found an enormous claw bone in a Surrey clay pit. When he took the claw to the Museum, experts realised that it belonged to a large meat-eating dinosaur – which they called Baryonyx, meaning 'heavy claw' (see above). Before this discovery, no one had known about this kind of dinosaur

Many of the specimens were collected by experts on expeditions to remote parts of the world – and even beyond, in space.

Moon rock, *collected by the Apollo XVII mission in 1972*

In 1985, many new kinds of insects were collected when Museum scientists went on an expedition to the rain forests of Indonesia. To reach insects high in the trees, scientists sprayed them with smoke guns. Insects then fell into funnel shaped nets and were taken back to the Museum for identification

Often a zoo or private owner will contact the Museum when an animal dies. If the animal is interesting or unusual, the Museum may then decide to take it and prepare it for display.

Giant pandas are among the rarest mammals in the world. In the wild, they are found only in the bamboo forests of western China. This giant panda, Chi-Chi, was brought from China to London Zoo. She died of old age on 22nd July 1972, and was given to the Museum. She can now be seen by visitors too young to have seen her alive

In 1930, the greyhound Mick the Miller held the British greyhound racing record of nineteen consecutive race wins. He was bred in Ireland by a priest called Father Brophy. When Mick died in 1938 his body was given to the Museum

Clouded leopard, *from India and Southeast Asia*

Simien jackal, *from Ethiopia*

Young snow leopard, *from Central Asia*

Young Javan tiger, *from Indonesia*

Young Chinese tiger

Maned wolf, *from South America*

Most of the large mammals in the Museum, such as the *bison*, were collected a long time ago. Today it is forbidden to hunt some of these mammals because they are in danger of becoming **extinct**.

The meat-eating mammals above are now protected by law.

Natural history on show

One of the main aims of the Museum is to display natural objects for visitors to see.

A display can be one of many things – a photograph, a film, a model or even a real object. The method of display chosen depends on what the animal, plant or mineral is like.

Many of the mammals and birds on show in the Museum are actual animals. The animals are no longer alive but they have been specially prepared by experts, called **taxidermists**, to make them *look* alive. Some people call these animals 'stuffed' but this is not how they are prepared. Many are actually hollow!

Mounting

This is how a Museum taxidermist might prepare a mammal for display...

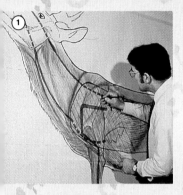

First, photographs of the animal are taken and measurements carefully recorded

Then the animal's skin is removed and put into a mixture of water, salt and acid, to preserve it

The 'body form' is made out of wire and finely shredded wood, called wood-wool. The wire is bent into the shape of the animal and sometimes the animal's own skull is attached to it

Then damp wood-wool is wrapped round the wire to make the body. Finer features are modelled out of **papier-mâché** and plaster. The measurements taken earlier are used to get the animal's shape exactly right so that the skin will fit properly

The animal's skin is then glued onto the 'body form'. This is called **mounting** the skin

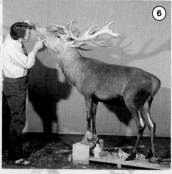

When the skin is in position, the seams can be carefully stitched together

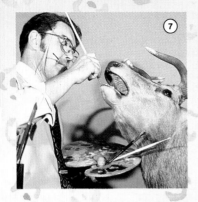

⑦ The soft parts of the animal, such as its nose or tongue, are modelled out of beeswax and painted. Glass eyes are added to make the animal look alive

When the mounted specimen is ready for display, it is usually put into a glass case along with a small plastic container of insecticide. This is to kill the carpet beetles which may get into the case and lay their eggs. The eggs hatch into larvae, called *woolly-bears*, which feed on the specimens.

Birds are prepared in much the same way. Taxidermists often paint the beaks and legs of birds because, with time, their colours fade.

13

Mammals

Mammals are animals that have hair or fur and produce milk for their young to feed on.

Human beings, dogs, mice, whales and dolphins are just a few of the thousands of different mammals.

Here are just some of the mounted mammal specimens on display at the Museum...

Giant anteaters live *in the forests and grasslands in Argentina and Central America. Although they live mainly on the ground they are also good swimmers. As well as ants, they eat termites, beetle grubs, and soft fruits*

This big African elephant *is a male from Malawi, in Africa. It is over 3 m (9.8 ft) high at the shoulder. The hole in its ear came from an old wound. The skin was probably torn by thorns*

Orangutans *have long fingers
and toes for gripping branches.
Because they have quick senses
and good eyesight, they
rarely fall*

Bats *are the only mammals
that can fly. Their long fingers are covered in a thin
layer of skin, to form a wing. This bat, the* Indian
flying fox, *feeds on ripe fruits*

The brown hare *lives on farm-
land, where it feeds on crops
and young trees. In spring, it
can often be seen chasing
and 'boxing', as part of a
spectacular courtship ritual*

The okapi *is a close relative
of the giraffe. It is a shy,
secretive animal that lives
deep in the African forests*

Birds

Birds are the only animals with feathers. Not all birds can fly but all have a beak, wings, scaly legs and feet, and tail feathers.

Hornbills *live in the dense jungles of Borneo*

Owls *feed on all sorts of animals – small mammals, insects, frogs and fish. They have especially soft feathers so they can fly without making a sound*

Penguins *are sea birds which live in the cold waters of the Antarctic. They cannot fly or walk very well but they are very good swimmers. They chase fast swimming fish and squid, which they eat*

Ostriches *are the largest birds in the world. Male ostriches can grow up to 2.5 m (8.2 ft) tall. They cannot fly but they have powerful legs and can run at speeds of up to 60 km (37.2 miles) an hour*

The scarlet ibis *is found in Central and South America. It uses its long curved beak to feed on small animals that live in shallow water and mud*

Peacocks *are male birds. They have very long, colourful feathers which they can raise into huge shimmering fans to attract female* peahens

Fishes, frogs, snakes ...and their relatives

Most of these creatures can be mounted, like mammals and birds, although the smaller specimens are usually modelled.

After mounting, these animals usually need to be painted because the colour of their skin fades. This is often very intricate work. Sometimes every fish scale has to be painted separately!

White-striped poison frogs – *poisonous extracts from the skins are used on the arrows of some South American Indians*

In order to get the colours exactly right, taxidermists usually take colour photographs of the animals before mounting.

This rare lungfish *lives in some of the rivers in Queensland, Australia. Using its lungs, it breathes by gulping air at the surface of the water*

Animals such as crocodiles, tortoises and turtles, snakes and lizards are **reptiles**. Here are some of the mounted reptile specimens on display in the Museum...

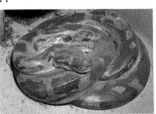

Rock pythons *can grow up to 6 m (19.7 ft) long. They sometimes feed on animals as large as deer or goats and can even eat porcupines*

The Komodo dragon, *the largest living lizard, lives on some of the Indonesian islands. This lizard can grow up to 3 m (9.8 ft) long. It feeds mainly on dead, rotting flesh, but has been known to attack and even kill humans*

The caiman, *a relative of the crocodile, comes from the Amazon region of South America. It feeds mainly on snails and fishes*

Models in the Museum

Not all animals can be mounted – it depends on how well their skins can be preserved. A taxidermist could not mount a jellyfish or giant squid because their skins are too watery. Nor could he mount **dinosaurs** because all we have left of them is their bones! So, to display these creatures, models are used.

Giant squids *live very deep in the sea. They can grow up to 18 m (59 ft) long – nearly as long as two buses! Squids move by squirting a jet of water through a hole below their heads, which pushes them forwards*

Dinosaurs

Dinosaurs lived on Earth millions of years ago. Although they died out over 65 million years ago, we know that they existed because their bones have been found preserved in rocks as **fossils**.

Experts compare the fossil bones with the bones of animals alive today, in order to build up a picture of what dinosaurs looked like.

With advice from fossil experts, modelmakers can then make models of dinosaurs and other extinct creatures such as *Archaeopteryx*, an ancient bird, and *pterosaurs*, which were sea reptiles.

Archaeopteryx, *which lived at the same time as some of the dinosaurs, was one of the first birds*

Not as fierce as it looks, Triceratops *was a plant-eater*

Modelmaking

Neanderthal people lived on Earth thousands of years ago. In the Museum there is a full-size model of a *neanderthal woman*. This was made by a Museum modelmaker, who based her shape on a 41 000 year old skeleton found in Israel.

Here you can see some of the stages of modelmaking...

1 Making drawings based on bone measurements

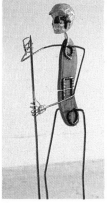

2 The finished framework, made from wood and steel wire

3 Building up the model with layers of sacking soaked in plaster

4 The model covered in Plasticine

5 Making a mould out of silicone rubber, for each side of the model

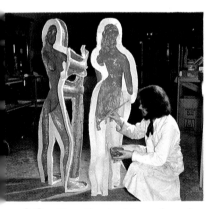

6 Coating the insides of each mould with protective gel, before lining with strengthened fibre glass and joining together

7 The painted model on display

The *blue whale* is one of the most famous models in the Museum. It took workmen about eighteen months to build.

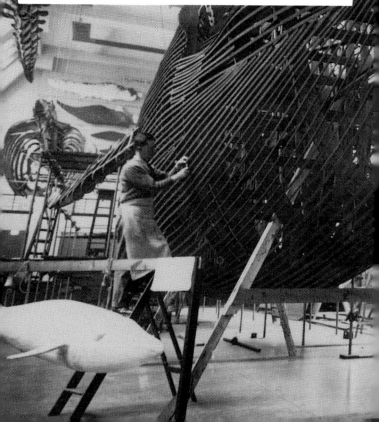

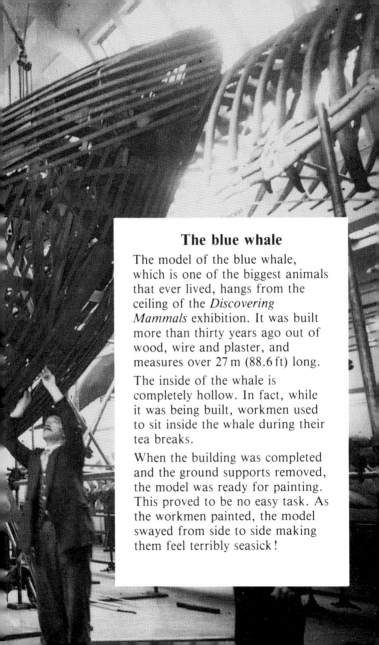

The blue whale

The model of the blue whale, which is one of the biggest animals that ever lived, hangs from the ceiling of the *Discovering Mammals* exhibition. It was built more than thirty years ago out of wood, wire and plaster, and measures over 27 m (88.6 ft) long.

The inside of the whale is completely hollow. In fact, while it was being built, workmen used to sit inside the whale during their tea breaks.

When the building was completed and the ground supports removed, the model was ready for painting. This proved to be no easy task. As the workmen painted, the model swayed from side to side making them feel terribly seasick!

Insects and spiders

In the Museum there are some giant-sized models
of mosquitoes, flies, butterflies and spiders.

*Modelmaker constructing the powerful pincers of
a giant scorpion – a close relative of the spider*

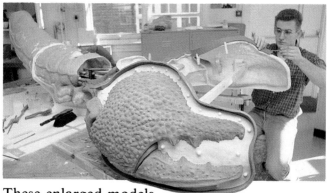

These enlarged models
enable the detail of these tiny creatures to be
seen more easily. But to give visitors an idea of
their proper size, real specimens are usually
placed next to the models.

Giant-sized models of a sandfly *(left)*
and a blackfly *(right)*

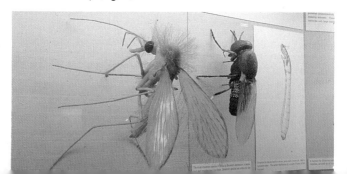

The inside story...

We can only see inside plants and animals by using special equipment. But in the Museum, models are used to show you...

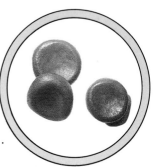

human blood cells...

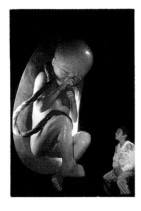

a baby in its mother's womb...

a human brain...

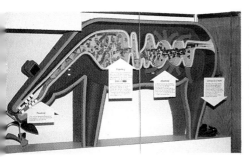

and the journey food makes through the four parts of a cow's stomach

Plants and fungi

Most of the plants and **fungi** in the Museum's displays are so lifelike that many people think they are living, growing things. In fact they are real but like many other specimens in the Museum, they are no longer alive.

Plants and fungi are usually frozen and then dried in a vacuum (freeze-dried). Afterwards, the specimens look and feel completely dry and can last in that condition for years.

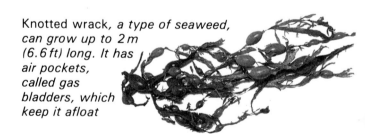

Parasol mushrooms *grow in grassy fields and on downland*

Knotted wrack, *a type of seaweed, can grow up to 2 m (6.6 ft) long. It has air pockets, called gas bladders, which keep it afloat*

In the natural world different plants, animals and other organisms live together in a variety of different surroundings, known as **habitats**.

In the *Ecology* exhibition, some of these habitats have been realistically created using models, mounted animals and other display techniques.

Underwater scene

This woodland setting contains a wide variety of plants, including ferns and horsetails, flowering plants, mosses, algae and lichens

Displaying fossils

Most fossils are very fragile so from the time they are found to finally putting them on display, they need to be handled with care.

In the field...
Experts wrap strips of material, dipped into plaster paste, round the fossil. When the plaster has set hard, the fossil is ready for its journey back to the Museum.

This fossilised dinosaur footprint, *found in Dorset, is about 135 million years old*

Woolly mammoth tooth, *about 50 000 years old, from Canada*

Back in the Museum...

The plaster jacket can be removed from the fossil by soaking it in water. But the fossil is still partly hidden by rock. One way of removing the rock is to chip at it with fine tools.

Another way is to use acid, which dissolves away the rock. Sometimes the actual fossil goes on display, but often a copy, a fossil **replica**, is displayed so that the real fossil can be studied by scientists.

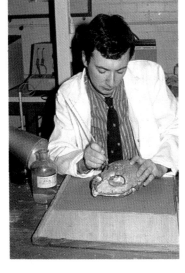

Fossil ammonite, *about 180 million years old, from Dorset*

To make a fossil replica, first, a mould of the real fossil is made and filled with fibre glass. Then, when the fibre glass has set hard, it is painted and varnished to make it look like the real specimen.

Making a replica of a fossil claw

This is a replica of Tyrannosaurus rex, *one of the fiercest dinosaurs. We can tell that it ate flesh because of its sharp, pointed teeth*

Its huge teeth could grow over 15 cm (6 inches) long

This replica of Diplodocus *was taken from actual bones found in Wyoming, in America. Diplodocus lived about 150 million years ago. At over 24m (78.7 ft) long, it is one of the largest animals ever known*

This fossil Ichthyosaurus *is about 185 million years old. Although it lived at the same time as some dinosaurs, Ichthyosaurus was a sea reptile, not a dinosaur. It probably fed on shellfish*

From inner Earth to outer space – minerals, rocks and meteorites

Unlike animals and plants, **minerals** are not living things. They are particles found naturally in the ground, many in rocks.

Apart from mercury, all minerals are solid. Some have special properties, which can be shown clearly when they are displayed.

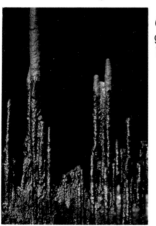

Glittering rods of the mineral goethite, *from Rossbach, West Germany*

This beautiful table top is made from ancient Roman marble

Gemstones are rare minerals which are especially beautiful and lasting. Today gemstones are mined in many areas of the world, particularly the Americas, Africa, Australia and Siberia. Usually they are cut and polished to show their full colour and shine.

Crystals of vanadinite, *a mineral found in Miblanden, Morocco*

Small pieces of planets from outer space are constantly heading towards Earth. Most of them burn up in the Earth's atmosphere but those that reach the surface are known as **meteorites**. About 3000 meteorites have been found around the world. Some of these are displayed in the Museum.

The Cranbourne meteorite, *which weighs 3.5 tonnes (3.4 tons) was found in Cranbourne, Australia in 1854. It is made of metal and would rust if left exposed to the air. To protect it, a gas called nitrogen is added to the air inside the case*

'Hands-on' displays

Usually the best way to learn about something is to do it! In the Museum today, there are many new **exhibitions** with 'hands-on' displays for visitors to try.

You can now...

pick up phones to hear the trumpeting of African and Indian elephants...

stand in a booth to experience your body's reaction to fright...

press a button to find out why you look the way you do...

and push buttons to see where your hormones – chemical messengers in your body – come from

These are just a few of the many 'hands-on' displays in the Museum. There are also many computer games to play and videos to watch.

Behind the scenes –
the Museum as a 'sorting house'

The Natural History Museum has a very important role to play in improving knowledge about the natural world around us.

The thousands of specimens on display for the public are only a tiny fraction of the Museum's collections. Behind the scenes – stored in countless boxes, bottles and drawers – are millions more specimens. Together, all these animals, plants and minerals form an enormous encyclopaedia of natural history, which must be carefully looked after.

The fishes in these jars are kept in ethanol to preserve them

Every year, thousands of new specimens pour into the Museum from all over the world. These all have to be sorted and identified. To do this,

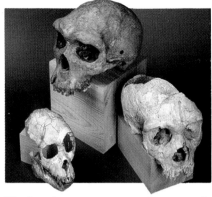

Skulls of our ancestors: Proconsul *(left) 18 million years old,* Rhodesian Man *(centre) 120 000 years old,* Neanderthal Man *(right) 70 000 years old*

there are more than 300 scientists working in the Museum. They sort into groups and give scientific names to all the different things we know of.

In the next few pages you can find out why identifying things is so important – and how this work could affect you.

The Museum is home to over 60 million kinds of natural things. All of these have to be labelled and catalogued

39

Identifying things

Every year, hundreds of packages arrive at the Museum from members of the public. Inside these packages, alive or dead, part or whole, are natural things that people have found. They send them to the Museum hoping to find out exactly what their specimen is.

In recent years the Museum has identified...

rat droppings, found in a packet of sesame seeds...

grain weevils, found in a sack of barley...

Quite often, the Museum is sent specimens that people have found in their food. In 1988, for example, the Museum received several packets of grapes, all bought from the same supermarket. Inside these packets there were large black spiders, which the Museum identified as dangerous *black widow spiders* from America.

a *rattlesnake backbone*, found in a packet of peanuts...

a *centipede*, found in a packet of French beans

Sorting out the souvenirs

It is illegal to bring souvenirs into this country which are made from animals or plants that are in danger of becoming extinct – such as tortoiseshell earrings, ivory spoons and lizard-skin wallets.

Many elephants are killed for their ivory tusks, which are then carved into ornaments and jewellery

Sometimes Customs officials may send a souvenir to the Natural History Museum, where scientists can identify whether or not it is made from an endangered animal.

To identify a product, scientists compare it with other specimens in the Museum's collections. This can be a very difficult job. A mammal is most easily identified by its head, tail or feet. But most mammal products, such as fur coats, are made only from the animal's

Wild cats such as this leopard are killed for their skins, which are then made into fur coats

body skin and often the skin has been dyed or cut into thin strips and sewn up again.

Products made from the skins of reptiles, such as crocodiles, lizards or snakes, are usually identified by looking at the pattern of the body scales.

Souvenirs identified as being made from endangered animals are confiscated, to discourage people from buying these products again.

43

Police work

Forensic scientists at the Museum help the police to examine evidence

Museum insect experts are sometimes called upon to help the police to investigate criminal cases.

For example, from the types of insects found squashed on a windscreen or trapped in the tread of a car's wheels, the experts can tell where the car has been. The number of insects can tell them the season of the year, the weather, and even the speed at which the car was travelling.

All this information might provide evidence to show that a particular car was in the area where a crime had been committed. This evidence could then lead to the conviction of the suspected criminal.

Solving mysteries

Sightings of monsters, dragons, kelpies and mermaids have been recorded over thousands of years through art and folklore. But do these, and other mysterious creatures, really exist?

The Natural History Museum is often consulted over reported sightings of unusual beasts, such as the *Loch Ness monster* in Scotland and the *yeti* in the Himalayas. But sightings are not enough for Museum scientists. To identify anything, they need a piece of the animal to study.

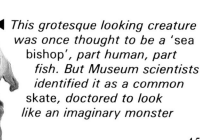

◀ *This grotesque looking creature was once thought to be a 'sea bishop', part human, part fish. But Museum scientists identified it as a common* skate, *doctored to look like an imaginary monster*

The Geological Museum

The Natural History Museum is part of a group of three museums which includes the *Geological Museum* in London and the *Zoological Museum* in Tring, Hertfordshire.

The Geological Museum, now linked to the Natural History Museum by a special gallery, is a treasure house of minerals, rocks and fossils – not only from Earth, but also from outer space.

Here you can...

admire one of the finest collections of gemstones in the world...

touch a button to make a model volcano erupt...

stand on a
lifesize model of
an offshore
drilling platform...

press buttons to
see which minerals
are used to make
everyday objects...

and even
star gaze

47

The Zoological Museum, Tring

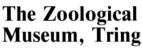

Red-collared lorikeet

The *Zoological Museum* in Tring was first opened to the public about one hundred years ago. Even today it has a lovely old-fashioned feel to it.

Here, there is a large variety of mounted animals on display, especially of birds and mammals.

Many of the specimens were donated by Lord Rothschild (1868-1937), who had a lifelong interest in collecting and studying natural history

Some of the mounted dogs *on display*

One of the highlights of the Museum is a unique display of mounted dogs. These dogs date from as early as 1843 to the present day. Many were once prize winners. Others, such as two *Afghans*, were the first dogs of their breed to be brought into Britain.

Looking at the very early specimens, it is amazing to see how some of the breeds of dog have changed. The *dachshund*, for example, looks very different from those of its breed alive today.

This dachshund *was presented to the Museum in 1912. It is much bigger than dachshunds of today*

49

Glossary

dinosaur a kind of reptile that lived on land millions of years ago

exhibition a display of objects

extinct died out

fossil the remains or traces of an animal or plant that have been preserved in rocks

fungi a group of organisms, including mushrooms and toadstools, that feed on dead and waste plant and animal material

habitat the type of place where a plant or animal naturally grows or lives

meteorite a fragment of rock or metal reaching Earth's surface from outer space

mineral a tiny particle found often in rock

mounting the placing of an animal's skin on a framework when preparing it for display

natural history the study of animals, plants and minerals

papier-mâché a modelling material made from a mixture of paper and glue

replica an exact copy

reptile a cold-blooded animal, such as a snake or lizard, that has a body covered in scales

specimen an animal, plant or mineral used for study

taxidermist a person who prepares and mounts the skins of animals to make the animals look lifelike

terracotta fine pottery that has not been glazed, which can be used as a building stone

Index

All in the Natural History Museum!

Hummingbird,
*the smallest bird
in the world*

Diamond,
the hardest mineral

Giant spider
crab, *the
largest crab*